How to make and fly model hot-air balloons

Gaily coloured hot-air balloons floating silently over the countryside are a magical sight we have come to welcome.

Now Ray Morse brings their grace and fascination within reach of enthusiasts of all ages by showing how to build and fly them as simple models. He has fully tested all these designs and uses inexpensive and readily available materials; so that even if you have little modelling skill you can get started with confidence. Find yourself a table-top and a quiet corner, read his helpful advice on tools and methods, and you'll soon be gazing up with delight and satisfaction at one of your own creations.

Ray Morse was born into an engineering family and during the Second World War was involved in aircraft instrument design. He has demonstrated some of his models on TV programmes and at exhibitions, and contributed frequently to aeronautical magazines in Great Britain, France and the United States.

How to make and fly model hot-air balloons

Ray Morse

John Murray

© Ray Morse 1978

Printed and bound in
Great Britain by
Redwood Burn Limited
Trowbridge and Esher

0 7195 3553 0

Contents

Introduction

Glancing up at the skies you may have been fortunate enough to see a modern hot-air balloon, with perhaps a crew of two or three, drifting serenely over the countryside, a majestic and colourful sight. After a lapse of almost 200 years, during which the gas balloon predominated, the hot-air balloon is now enjoying a big revival both in this country and abroad. Much credit for this popularity is due to the efforts made in the United States in the early 1950s, together with the use of propane as a convenient fuel. You may have been to one of the numerous balloon meetings organized in various parts of the country and witnessed the inflation and flying techniques by the club members. If, however, you have not been fortunate enough to participate in full-scale ballooning and your pocket is not very deep, why not try the next best thing – building your own model lighter-than-air (LTA) craft, not necessarily a static exhibition model, but one that can actually fly? Model balloons are quick and cheap to build, can provide hours of pleasure, and one has the added satisfaction of making something unique. Perhaps you have viewed the fine display of model airships and balloons at the Science Museum, South Kensington, London? You will be well repaid by a visit to exhibitions of this nature and you will glean a fair amount of knowledge on LTA craft (or aerostats) both as regards design and construction.

As far as I am aware, this is the first volume to be published on the subject of flying model hot-air balloons, although from time to time occasional booklets and magazines have appeared containing the odd chapter here and there amongst other subjects, such as planes, boats and kites. I trust, therefore, that this book will lead to many colourful balloon models floating skyward in the near future.

I can guarantee that all the examples in this book will operate satisfactorily as I have put many hours of work into their development.

As a consequence of the recent steep increase in the cost of helium and the extreme danger of using hydrogen gas, on account of its highly explosive nature when mixed with air, I do not recommend the gas balloon for the enthusiast. Utilizing hot air as a lifting agent, danger problems are dispensed with and you can get airborne with methylated spirits as heating fuel for only a few pence. I have conducted many successful tests with gas-filled models, but projects of this kind would be more suitable for a joint effort, such as in a school or club, where resources could be pooled to purchase gas and pay for cylinder rental. Therefore, for economic reasons, I recommend the hot-air balloon, which is cheap and simple to build from readily obtainable materials, with methylated spirits to provide the hot air as the lifting agent.

A corner of the author's workshop showing balloons and templates on wall, with tools and materials on bench.

Chapter 1
Your Factory

Try to avoid a temporary site for your balloon
factory, such as the kitchen worktop or the
sitting-room floor. Aim at a separate den, a
disused garage or loft which could be adapted.
You may, of course, have a garden shed or
outhouse, though here heating could pose a
problem.

For small or close work, artificial lighting in
the form of a strip light above the bench,
together with an adjustable Anglepoise-type
lamp, make an ideal combination for dark
evenings, though a large window allowing
natural daylight is to be preferred. Some
people find strip lighting rather hard to work
by. In this case, fit standard 80- or 100-watt
bulbs with suitable shades to combat the glare.

Having selected your site and settled lighting
methods, focus attention on the bench – port-
able or collapsible affairs are not suitable. I
recommend a permanent built-in structure,
wall-to-wall if possible so as to obtain the maximum length for template cutting and balloon
assembly. The bench framing need not be too
heavy, but do cover the top with a smooth
board, such as three-ply or 'Royal' hard-
board. A 230-volt 13-amp power point is
almost essential for the serious builder situ-
ated near the bench, thus enabling you to plug
in various electric tools. A small to medium-

size vice is practically indispensable and enables you to hold timber or metal for cutting and acts as an aid when forming wire parts.

Fortunately for us, the costly lathe or milling machine as used by mechanical engineers are not essential. All that is required is a set of small hand-tools which can be obtained at very reasonable prices at most large department stores. Listed below are the tools I find most useful:

    Saws for wood and metal
    Small hammer
    Set of files
    Set of screwdrivers
    Centre punch
    Pair of scissors
    Pair of flat-nose pliers
    Pair of round-nose pliers
    Pair of metal snips
    Sanding blocks
    Backed razor blades
    Balsa cutters
    Needle awl
    Brace
    Set of twist drills
    Paint brushes
    Set of drawing instruments

You can, of course, get by on nearly all the work without power tools, but where speed and output are prime factors, they are a great aid. Below are the main electric tools which I find of most assistance:

    Drill
    Circular saw

Plastic welder/cutter
Soldering bit
Paint spray

In your workshop it will be a help to build up a supply of sandpaper, solder and fluxes, adhesive tapes, twine, cotton, fine wire, glue and paints. The stock of actual building materials depends largely on the jobs you have in mind. I usually endeavour to buy more than I need and thus avoid running out of supplies at a crucial moment.

Shelves, racks and even discarded bookcases around the walls will accommodate most of your materials. A cabinet with drawers is very useful for smaller parts and for keeping them away from dust. I use empty screw-cap glass jars for holding screws, washers, pins, etc., each labelled for easy identification.

Modellers vary in their choice of tools. Many work well with small planes and chisels, though I rarely use them. Organizing a tool department is not a bad training, ballooning or not! There are always numerous jobs needing attention and tools are an investment that pay a bonus.

Chapter 2
Flying Methods

There are many records of gas-filled toy balloons travelling hundreds of miles. One is even reputed to have drifted across the Atlantic from Wales to California! I have had several exciting replies from different places in England and one address label returned from West Germany for which I won a prize organized by a local fête. However, with hot-air ballooning there is not nearly so much risk of losing a valuable model due, of course, to the limit of the heating fuel. One of my prized relics of pre-war days is a 3-ft blue and white paper balloon which drifted across a Sussex common from a garden party at Smalldole, a small hamlet near the South Downs. There was a light wind and the model had only travelled some 2 miles before the methylated spirits was expended. I remember racing down the lane in the late afternoon of that summer's day to the big house at the foot of the hill, occupied by relatives of Wilberforce of slave abolition fame, and begged them for the balloon now lying partially deflated in the meadows behind, surrounded by a herd of particularly curious cows!

However, before releasing any balloon you should have some idea where it may land (a) in order to retrieve it and (b) to avoid disturbing other people by landing on private property. Always remember not to fly near an aerodrome, factory or motorway. For long-distance flights it's sensible to secure a note in the gondola giving your name and address, time and place of launch, requesting return should you fail to locate it.

When flying hot-air balloons with burners, it is never advisable to tether them, as even in the slightest wind the canopy will tilt and most likely the fabric will catch alight. In some countries, e.g. the United States, one is forbidden by law to carry a fire aloft. However, much pleasure can be gained by holding the model over a small picnic or camping stove, preferably with a metal chimney, to conduct the hot air, releasing when a good lift is felt. An old friend of mine, Francis Boreham, has told me of an even simpler experiment. One day, he acquired a large plastic laundry bag which he filled over a bonfire in the garden. Upon releasing it, it shot skyward, eventually descending in a neighbour's garden. Of course, flight times are limited, but I have myself 'jumped' a small 18-in. diameter balloon repeatedly over a two-storey house to land it on the back lawn. Frequent competitions have been held in the United States for long duration, some very considerable, simply by using a heating appliance on the ground. Not only boys enter these competitions but girls, many of whom have often walked off with the prizes!

Always inflate hot-air balloons in a sheltered spot near a building, hedge or trees, clear of obstacles downwind. Get several helpers to hold out the limp balloon to the approximate shape before lighting the burner, then wait until there is a definite upward pull before releasing. In this 'light' condition, as it is called, the model should soon ascend. Fortunately, with hot-air balloons, length of flight can be determined by quantity of fuel used, remembering that you normally reach your ceiling when fuel is exhausted and that the drift may take your model a considerable distance further downwind before it reaches the ground again. Always time the burner duration by a 'bench test' first. It's surprising how rapidly a model will disappear, even in a light wind, so limit your methylated spirits carefully. Never use petrol or paraffin. I once tried the former in the burner of a 9-ft balloon. The blowlamp-like roar would have done justice to a Boeing 707. It was a miracle I had any hair or eyebrows left! Lesson learned. It made me cautious of fire. When filling burner, I always use a small measure to give the length of burn required. Spilt methylated spirits can be dangerous, especially in areas of dry grass or scrub which can readily be set alight and cause untold damage to crops or wildlife. Please see, too, that matches are spent before throwing away. Metal foil chimneys over burners will protect tissue paper from the flames.

Chapter 3
A Very Simple Balloon

Crown
Centre line
Crease
Skirt

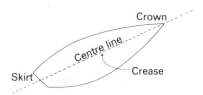

Fig 1 Template material brown paper

If you wish to get airborne quickly, why not try your hand at this simplest of balloons as a basic first effort? Purchase some lightweight tissue paper from your local store. You can use model aircraft covering, such as Modelspan, but for hot-air balloons the ordinary commercial grade is quite suitable. You can obtain most colours. Packets cost only a few pence. Select contrasting colours such as orange/blue, green/yellow, blue/yellow. Most colours agree with white. You may prefer a single colour, but contrasting alternate panels (gores) look best.

Centre line crease

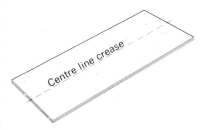

Fig 2 Pile of tissues

Centre line crease
Template
Tissue pile

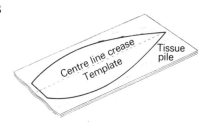

Fig 3 Template on pile of tissue paper, pin together

2 tissue gores ready for seaming
Top panel
Offset app. $\frac{1}{4}$ in.
Lower panel

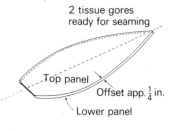

Fig 4 Two-tissue gores ready for seaming

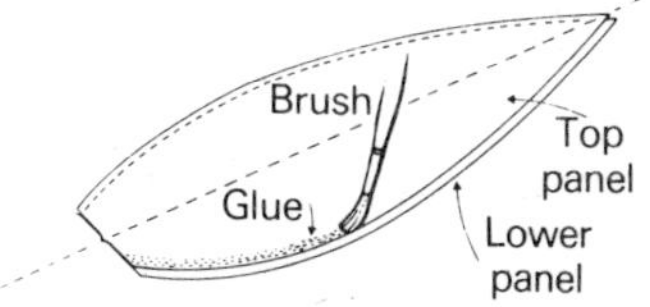

Brush
Top panel
Glue
Lower panel
Run glue along edge of top panel. Fold lower projecting edge up over on to it, thus forming seam

Fig 5 Seaming

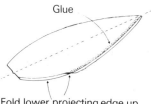

Glue
Fold lower projecting edge up on to glued edge of top panel

Fig 6 Seaming

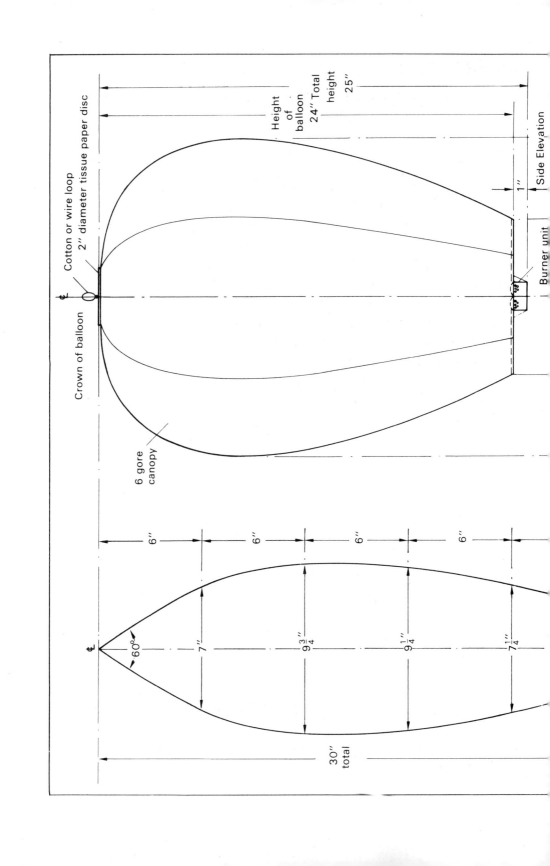

Crown of balloon

Cotton or wire loop
2" diameter tissue paper disc

Height
of
balloon
24" Total
height
25"

Side Elevation

1"

Burner unit

6 gore
canopy

6"
6"
6"
6"

60°

7"
9¾"
9¼"
7¼"

30"
total

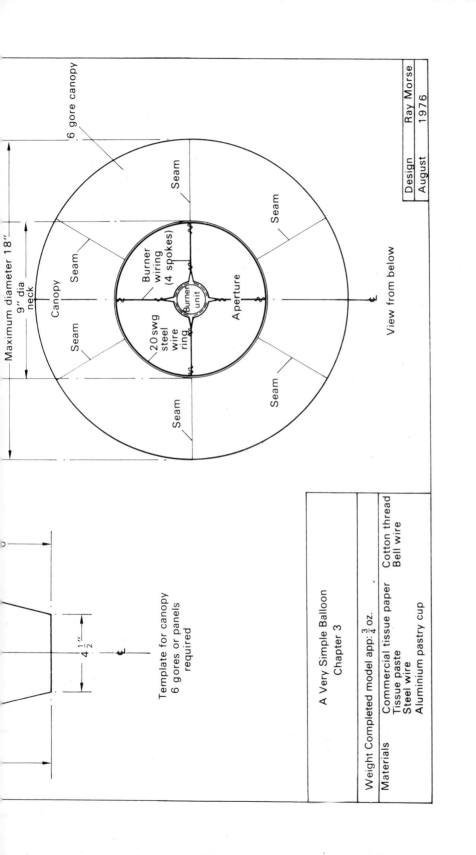

6 gore canopy

Seam

Seam

Seam

Maximum diameter 18″

9″ dia neck

Canopy

Seam

Seam

Burner wiring (4 spokes)

Burner unit

20 swg steel wire ring

Aperture

Seam

Seam

Seam

View from below

$4\frac{1}{2}''$

Template for canopy
6 gores or panels
required

A Very Simple Balloon
Chapter 3

Weight Completed model app: $\frac{3}{4}$ oz.

Materials	Commercial tissue paper	Cotton thread
	Tissue paste	Bell wire
	Steel wire	
	Aluminium pastry cup	

Design	Ray Morse
August	1976

Start by cutting out a stiff template – thick brown wrapping paper is ideal. Fold it down the centre lengthwise to get shape uniform. Prepare six strips of tissue, 30 in. long, 10 in. wide. Crease each of these down the centre also, as template. This will aid assembly later. Stack them neatly in a pile with template on top, then pin the lot together temporarily. Following the shape of the template cut out the pile of tissues. Next, lay one panel flat on a smooth worktop, lay another on top offset sideways as shown by approx. $\frac{1}{4}$ in., then run glue along one edge of top panel and fold lower projecting edge over on to it, thus making the seam, which when opened later gives a strong lap join.

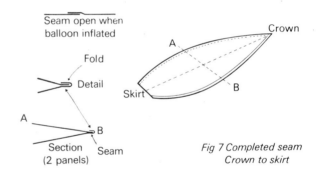

Seam open when balloon inflated

Fold

Detail

Section (2 panels) Seam

Skirt

Crown

Fig 7 Completed seam
Crown to skirt

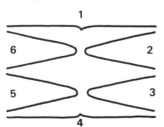

Fig 8a Panels assembled as
above (section) concertina
fashion

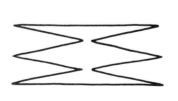

Fig 8b Collapsed balloon
(section) as assembled

Fig 8c Collapsed balloon as
viewed from crown

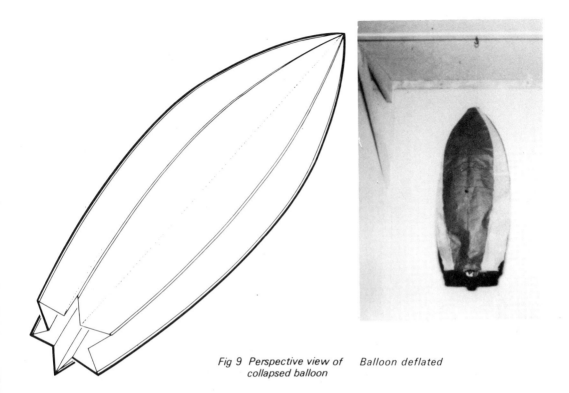

Fig 9 Perspective view of   Balloon deflated
     collapsed balloon

Assemble all six panels in pairs first, finally
assembling the resulting three pairs to make
the complete balloon. Study the diagrams
closely. Be careful to fold back completed
seams out of the way when gluing. Upon completion, open out immediately to ensure no
surplus glue is holding in the wrong place.
When dry, cut a 2-in. disc of tissue and glue to
crown, together with a small cotton loop,
handy to hold during inflation.

A simple ring of 22 swg steel or aluminium
wire will serve to keep the neck open, and will
also weight the balloon, otherwise it may tilt
in flight and spill the hot air before rising very
far.

21

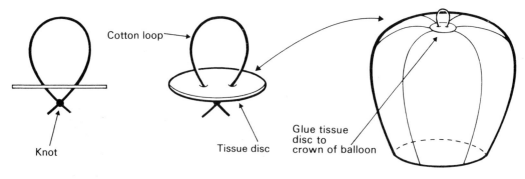

Cotton loop

Knot

Tissue disc

Glue tissue disc to crown of balloon

Fig 10

You are now ready for your maiden flight. Get a friend to hold the model by the cotton loop, making sure the balloon is opened to approximate shape, hold neck steadily over a small picnic or camping stove, and watch the balloon take shape. When you feel an upward tug, let go and, if all is well, you are in for an exciting flight. Should you desire greater duration and you live in a country where regulations permit fires to be carried aloft, fit a dis-

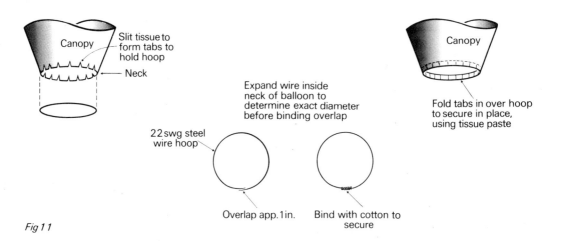

Canopy

Slit tissue to form tabs to hold hoop

Neck

Expand wire inside neck of balloon to determine exact diameter before binding overlap

22 swg steel wire hoop

Overlap app. 1 in.

Bind with cotton to secure

Canopy

Fold tabs in over hoop to secure in place, using tissue paste

Fig 11

carded aluminium foil pie container as a burner, adapted as shown, supported across the neck by four 'spokes' of bell wire. Fuel up with a teaspoon of methylated spirits, then up into the blue!

Fig 12 Burner unit

Pastry cup
Base diam. app. $1\frac{1}{2}$ in.
Top diam. app. 2 in.
Height $\frac{3}{4}$ in. to 1 in.

Empty pastry cup
(aluminium)

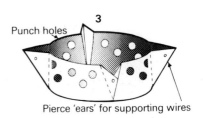

Pinch sides to form 4 'ears'

$\frac{3}{4}$ in. high

Punch holes

Pierce 'ears' for supporting wires

Punch holes

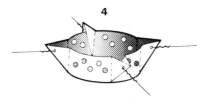

Attach 4 wires
(bell wire)

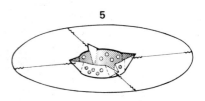

Attach burner to hoop
4 radial wires spoke fashion

Picnic stove for hot-air
Pole to hold balloon by loop

Fig 13 The very simple model about to lift off

Chapter 4
A 1930s Balloon

The tempting aroma of hot sizzling sausages hung in the air outside. Cooking was taking place in the crisp autumn evening. It was dark, and the boys at the Sussex coaching college had just had a splendid firework display, for it was Guy Fawkes Night. The sulphurous smell of spent fireworks mingled with the contents in the frying pans. Just one more item to round off the event: a hot-air balloon. Some of the boys mounted a tall stepladder whilst the Head, other tutors and boys stood by in the lee of the old Georgian mansion. The red and white monster expanded when the tow wick was lit and soon, amid cheers, the bright object had crossed the iron railings and over the road, mounting rapidly.

Left 1930s balloon deflated
Right 1930s balloon fully inflated

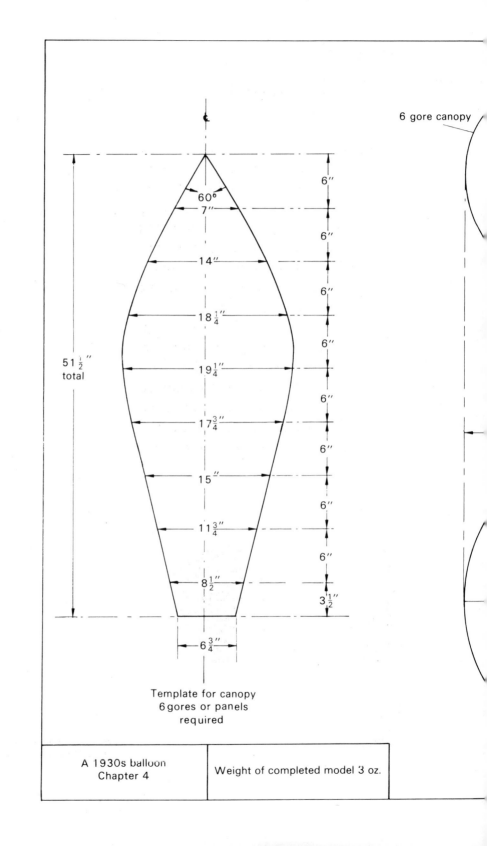

¢

60°

7"

14"

18 1/4"

19 1/4"

17 3/4"

15"

11 3/4"

8 1/2"

51 1/2"
total

6"

6"

6"

6"

6"

6"

6"

6"

3 1/2"

6 3/4"

Template for canopy
6 gores or panels
required

6 gore canopy

A 1930s balloon
Chapter 4

Weight of completed model 3 oz.

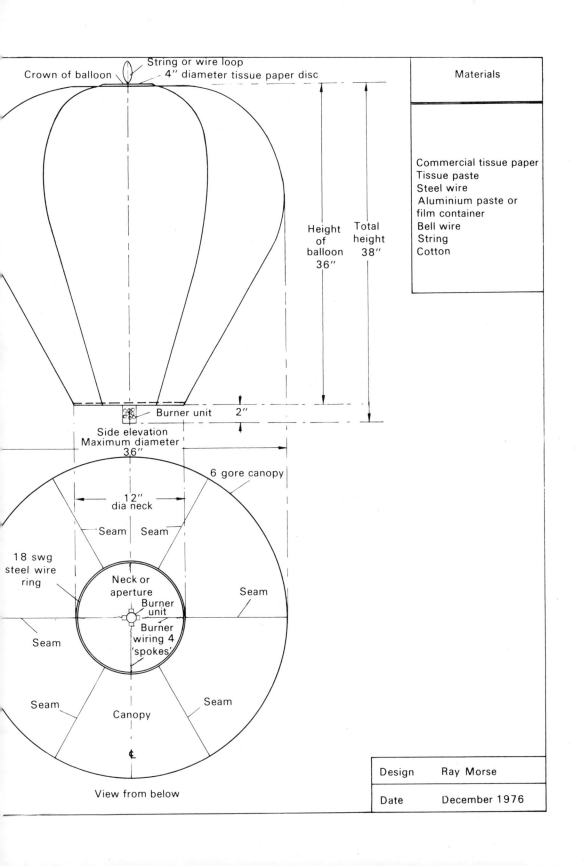

String or wire loop

Crown of balloon

4" diameter tissue paper disc

Height of balloon 36"

Total height 38"

Burner unit 2"

Side elevation
Maximum diameter 36"

Materials

Commercial tissue paper
Tissue paste
Steel wire
Aluminium paste or film container
Bell wire
String
Cotton

6 gore canopy

12" dia neck

Seam   Seam

18 swg steel wire ring

Neck or aperture
Burner unit
Burner wiring 4 'spokes'

Seam

Seam

Seam

Seam   Seam

Canopy

View from below

Design	Ray Morse
Date	December 1976

Alas, the spectacle was short-lived. A stronger current may have caught it, anyway, it suddenly burst into flame, not a fragment remaining alight before falling to ground!

In pre-war days, this pear-shaped type of balloon, some 3–4 ft diameter, was available at most stores stocking equipment for fêtes, parties, and other outdoor celebrations.

If you feel inclined to roll up your shirt-sleeves for this job, you will find it little more

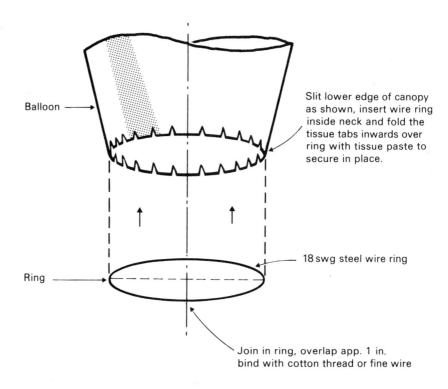

Balloon

Slit lower edge of canopy as shown, insert wire ring inside neck and fold the tissue tabs inwards over ring with tissue paste to secure in place.

18 swg steel wire ring

Ring

Join in ring, overlap app. 1 in. bind with cotton thread or fine wire

Fig 14 Wire ring

work than the model described in the previous chapter. Basically, it is just the same as regards construction, but offers much more scope for experiment due to its much greater lift. If you cannot obtain tissue long enough for the panels, you will need to join two sheets with a glued lap join of approx. $\frac{1}{2}$-in. overlap to make a strong seam. Otherwise, follow constructional details as explained in Chapter 3. The wire ring can be of 18 swg steel wire, and burner an empty paste container (aluminium) 2-in. high, 2-in. diameter with two or three

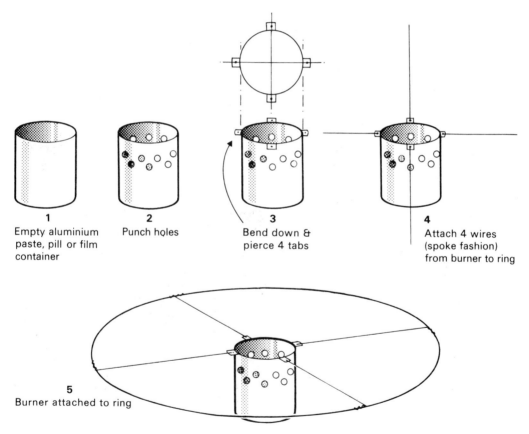

1
Empty aluminium paste, pill or film container

2
Punch holes

3
Bend down & pierce 4 tabs

4
Attach 4 wires (spoke fashion) from burner to ring

5
Burner attached to ring

Fig 15 Assembly of burner unit

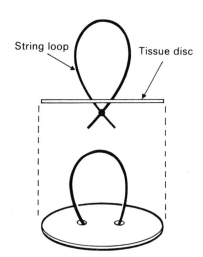

String loop

Tissue disc

rows of holes round the upper half to aid combustion. The more holes you punch in the container, the more air you will get to the methylated spirits. If you do not punch any holes, the flame will only burn sluggishly. The crown of the balloon can be reinforced with a 4-in. diameter tissue disc with string loop for holding or suspension. A bamboo cane or dowel rod with a hook or nail at the top is

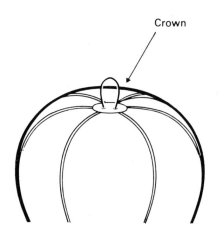

Crown

Fig 16 Tissue disc & loop at crown of balloon

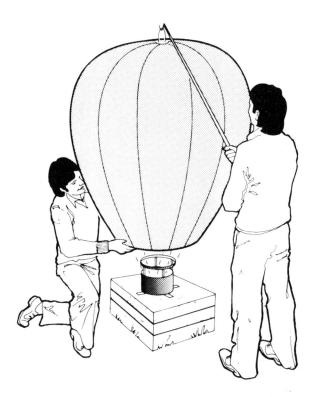

Fig 17 1930 s balloon about to ascend.
(This may be flown with or without burner unit)

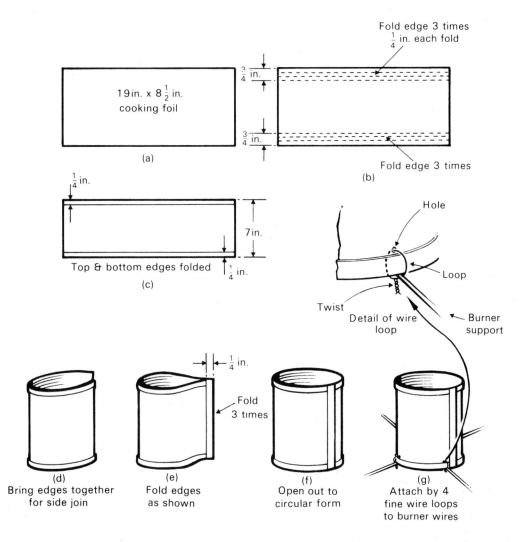

Fold edge 3 times
$\frac{1}{4}$ in. each fold

$\frac{3}{4}$ in.

19in. x 8$\frac{1}{2}$ in.
cooking foil

$\frac{3}{4}$ in.

(a)

Fold edge 3 times

(b)

$\frac{1}{4}$ in.

7in.

Top & bottom edges folded $\frac{1}{4}$ in.

(c)

Hole

Loop

Twist

Detail of wire
loop

Burner
support

$\frac{1}{4}$ in.

Fold
3 times

(d)
Bring edges together
for side join

(e)
Fold edges
as shown

(f)
Open out to
circular form

(g)
Attach by 4
fine wire loops
to burner wires

Fig 18 Chimney plan
   Suitable for 1930s balloon or Fiery Queen

ideal for supporting the model during inflation. The simple 'optional' foil chimney is worth its weight if you want to avoid an aerial conflagration! Name and address on board is not a bad habit to adopt. You never know!

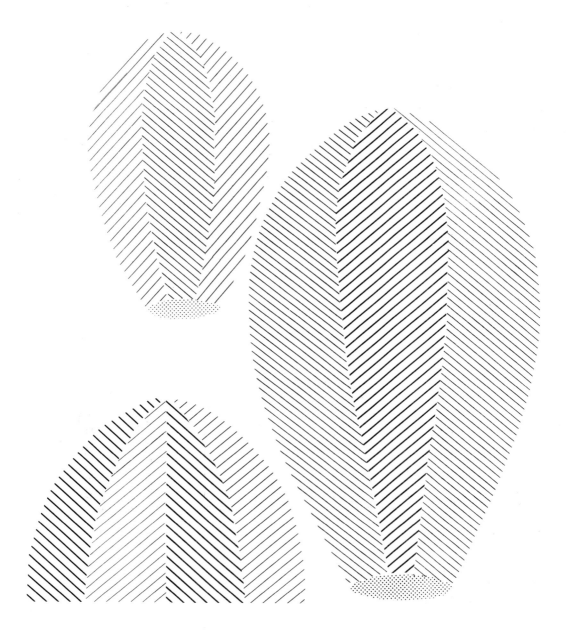

Chapter 5
Fiery Queen

The modern hot-air balloon makes an attractive subject. As your next attempt, why not add this near-scale model of the London Balloon Club's *Fiery Queen* to your collection?

The advantage of this design lies in the use of the rigid frame I have incorporated at the skirt. When inflating, you merely suspend the model, light up and it fills itself. No need to get assistance to hold the canopy out, as with the simpler models, since the frame keeps the fire well away from the fabric, so it's worth the additional work involved.

 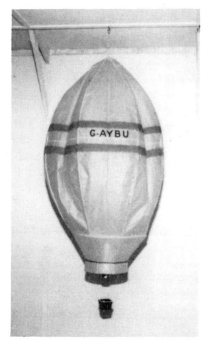

Left Fiery Queen deflated
Right Fiery Queen partially deflated

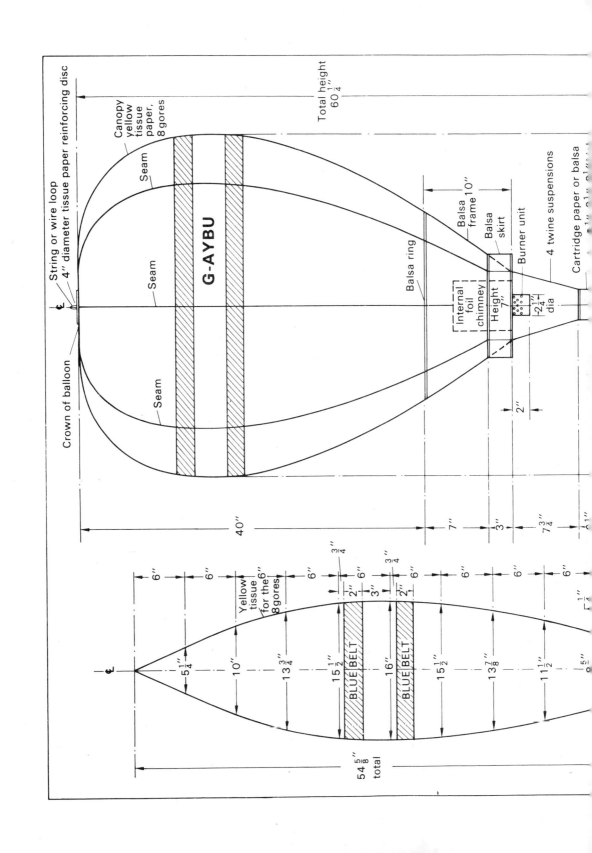

String or wire loop

4" diameter tissue paper reinforcing disc

Canopy
yellow
tissue
paper,
8 gores

Seam

Seam

Seam

Seam

Total height 60 $\frac{1}{4}$"

G-AYBU

Crown of balloon

Balsa ring

Internal foil chimney

Balsa frame 10"

Balsa skirt

Burner unit

Height 7"

4 twine suspensions

Cartridge paper or balsa

2 $\frac{1}{4}$" dia

40"

7"

3"

7 $\frac{3}{4}$"

2"

Yellow tissue for the 8 gores

6"

6"

6"

6"

$\frac{3}{4}$"

2"

6"

3"

6"

$\frac{3}{4}$"

2"

6"

6"

6"

6"

5 $\frac{1}{4}$"

10"

13 $\frac{3}{4}$"

15 $\frac{1}{2}$"

BLUE BELT

16"

BLUE BELT

15 $\frac{1}{2}$"

13 $\frac{7}{8}$"

11 $\frac{1}{2}$"

54 $\frac{5}{8}$" total

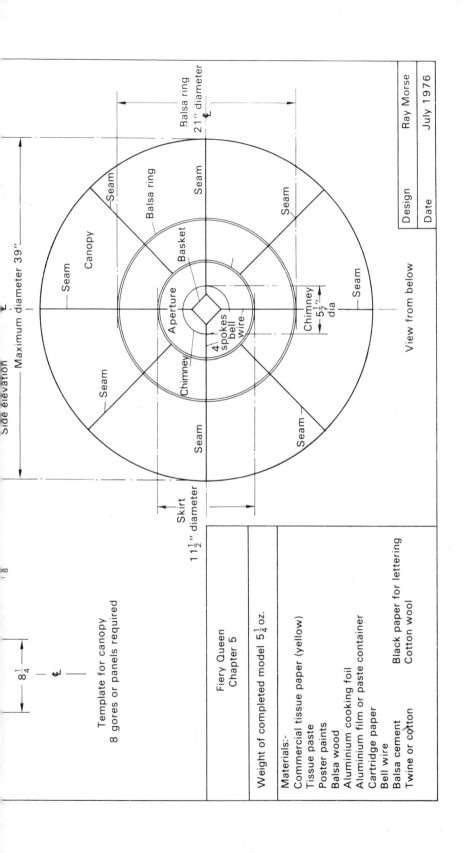

Side elevation

Maximum diameter 39"

Template for canopy
8 gores or panels required

$8\frac{1}{4}$

Balsa ring
21" diameter

Seam

Balsa ring

Canopy

Seam

Seam

Basket

Aperture

Seam

Chimney

$5\frac{1}{2}$"
dia

Chimney

4 spokes
bell
wire

Seam

Seam

Seam

Seam

Skirt
$11\frac{1}{2}$" diameter

View from below

Design	Ray Morse
Date	July 1976

Fiery Queen
Chapter 5

Weight of completed model $5\frac{1}{4}$ oz.

Materials:-
Commercial tissue paper (yellow)
Tissue paste
Poster paints
Balsa wood
Aluminium cooking foil
Aluminium film or paste container
Cartridge paper
Bell wire
Balsa cement   Black paper for lettering
Twine or cotton   Cotton wool

Stock up with a supply of yellow coloured tissue paper, enough for the eight-gore canopy. You will also need a few sticks of balsa for the frame.

Start as usual by cutting out a stiff brown paper template then, having glued up the panels to give required length, crease them down centre and pin together with template on top. It will not matter if you puncture the tissue with very small holes. This is not a gas balloon and any minute leak will be of little consequence. Cut out the pile, following the curvature of the template, of course. When separated, lay two panels flat on your bench

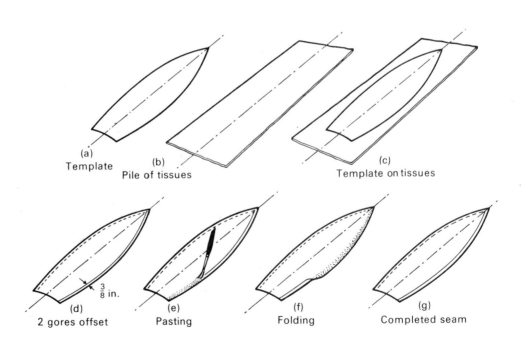

(a) Template   (b) Pile of tissues   (c) Template on tissues

(d) 2 gores offset $\frac{3}{8}$ in.   (e) Pasting   (f) Folding   (g) Completed seam

Fig 19 Canopy of Fiery Queen

36

offsetting them sideways by approx. $\frac{3}{8}$ in. as shown, then run glue along one edge of top panel and fold projecting edge of lower panel over on to it, forming the seam. Study the figures carefully. Assemble the panels first in pairs, the eight panels, of course, making four pairs which in turn glue together to form complete canopy. Open out immediately after using glue in case anything is stuck in the wrong place, and fix a 4-in. diameter disc at the crown with a string loop attached for suspending during inflation.

Next, build up the balsa frame and attach burner by four radial wires as shown, then

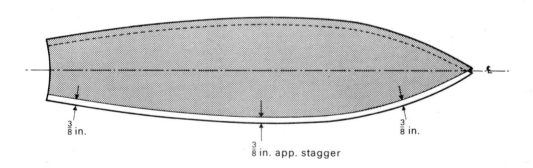

$\frac{3}{8}$ in.

$\frac{3}{8}$ in.

$\frac{3}{8}$ in. app. stagger

Fig 20 Canopy of Fiery Queen
Detail of two gores offset ready for pasting

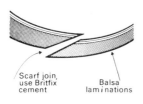

Scarf join,
use Britfix
cement

Balsa
laminations

a

Obtain large can or oil drum to
approx. diameter required,
preferably slightly larger than
ring diameter

Fig 21 Upper ring

b

Wrap balsa ring round drum,
using $\frac{1}{32}$ in. thick material, overlap
and join with Britfix. Wrap
another balsa ring over first,
cementing together, to form
laminations

Total 3 laminations

c

Repeat adding laminations
until required thickness is
built up. Allow cement to
harden overnight. Cut ring
and scarf, join to exact
diameter

cover the skirt and frame, using same type of tissue as for main canopy. Finally, carefully glue lower edge of canopy to top balsa ring on the frame, making sure the two diameters, the frame and canopy coincide. It may help to pin or clip the two units together at this stage whilst busy with the glue. For added realism, a light paper basket and 'crew' may be suspended below the burner. Make certain not to

Fig 22 Lower ring (skirt)

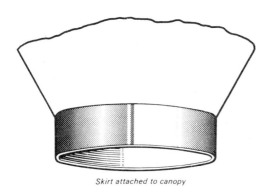

Skirt attached to canopy

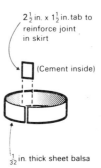

$2\frac{1}{2}$ in. x $1\frac{1}{2}$ in. tab to
reinforce joint
in skirt

(Cement inside)

$\frac{1}{32}$ in. thick sheet balsa

38

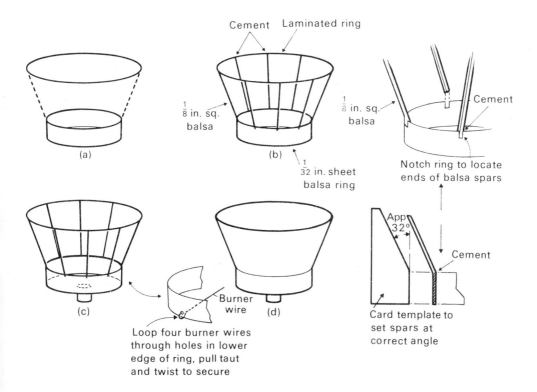

Cement   Laminated ring

$\frac{1}{8}$ in. sq. balsa

(a)

(b)

$\frac{1}{32}$ in. sheet balsa ring

Cement

$\frac{1}{8}$ in. sq. balsa

Notch ring to locate ends of balsa spars

(c)

Loop four burner wires through holes in lower edge of ring, pull taut and twist to secure

Burner wire

(d)

App. 32°

Cement

Card template to set spars at correct angle

Fig 23 Fiery Queen frame assembly and burner unit
Burner: same pattern as for 1930s model (Fig 15)
Chimney: same pattern as for 1930s model (Fig 18)

spill methylated spirits on to it, otherwise your model may create a bigger blaze than it bargained for! Two Thetford friends once drifted a small model with paper crew over a crowded football ground. It is not recorded that the event stopped play, but I understand that many of the spectators believed it to be the full-size thing crossing the skies above their heads!

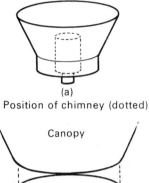

(a)

Position of chimney (dotted)

Canopy

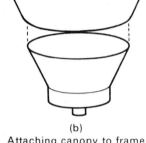

(b)

Attaching canopy to frame

Hold in place on top ring with pins or small bulldog clips whilst pasting the units together. Make sure the two diameters agree

Miniature crew or 'ballast' may be stowed in basket

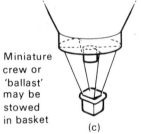

(c)

For added realism suspend a lightweight card or balsa basket below burner. Attach to the four burner wires, making certain length of all cords agree

Fig 24

If you have some patience left before your first flight and a flair for artistic things, you may embellish the canopy with two circumferential bands of blue (use poster paints, available at any art shop) and add the registration number in black. Back up the tissue with blotting paper or old newspapers inside to save staining the other side of the balloon. If you are not much of a hand at signwriting, try cutting letters from thin paper and stick on.

You are now ready for a trial flight. *Fiery Queen* can be tested in the garage first, if you like, but if outside, choose a near calm day and some shelter in the lee of a wall or hedge. Get a helper to suspend the model by the loop, from a pole fitted with a hook or nail at the top, sufficient to hold the model yet easy to disengage when it rises. Be careful not to jerk the model, else liquid fuel may spill over. Always fill from a measure or a small squeeze bottle with spout. Ignite with a match through a burner hole. After a few seconds the balloon will fill to shape, and soon after you will notice the lift develop. Immediately release the hook and away *Fiery Queen* will go into her element, continuing to rise for approximately one minute before descent begins. Allow plenty of space downwind to avoid obstacles when landing, but be prepared for a long chase. Happy landings!

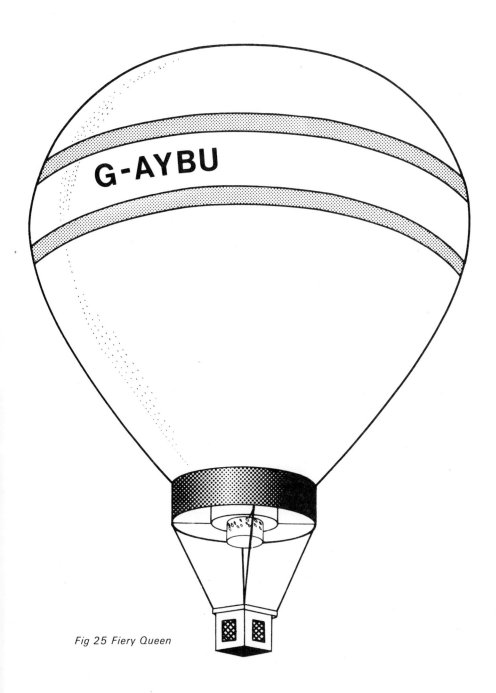

G-AYBU

Fig 25 Fiery Queen

Chapter 6
Rocket Balloon

(a) Join eight 20 in. x 30 in. sheets of tissue with approx $\frac{1}{4}$ in. overlap for seams

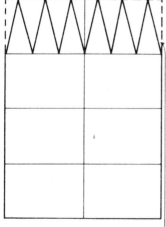

Red	Red
20 in. x 30 in.	20 in. x 30 in.
20 in. x 30 in.	20 in. x 30 in.
20 in. x 30 in.	20 in. x 30 in.
20 in. x 30 in.	20 in. x 30 in.

(b) Cut red panels as indicated to form the nose cone

Fig 26 Developed drawing of Rocket body

This simple but rather novel design can be completed in a matter of two to three hours, using basically inexpensive materials, and no more than a dessertspoon of methylated spirits to send it literally rocketing skyward. Due to the shape, it will rise rapidly to quite a considerable altitude, so why not surprise your friends at the local park with your own moon-shot! It certainly looks very convincing, especially from a distance.

In those countries where the law does not permit fires to be carried aloft, this model may be inflated quite satisfactorily over a small gas picnic stove so, should you indulge in weekend camping, take the model along. You will find out a lot about wind currents and direction.

There is no need to cut a template for this job – simply select a smooth, flat surface and join up the panels as indicated on the plan, lapping the tissue approx. $\frac{1}{4}$ in. White tissue with red nose looks well in the air. Having allowed the assembled panels to dry, lap and glue the cylindrical section, then carefully glue nose section. Gently open out as usual in case anything is sticking in the wrong place and add a reinforcing disc with string loop at the top for easy suspension during inflation. At this stage, you may wish to add realism by painting a name or number on the rocket, using poster paints as supplied by most art shops. For this, dark blue or black looks well. Back up the tissue inside with blotting paper or old newspapers to save staining the opposite surface, and keep the tissue still until dry to avoid smearing.

If you are flying without fire, make up a simple hoop of balsa or reed cane as shown and, having checked the diameter carefully, insert inside the lower edge of the rocket and fold the tissue over the hoop gluing this in place around the circumference. If carrying a fire aloft, continue by assembling the burner unit, finally mounting the complete ready-covered assembly to the rocket itself. Four polystyrene vanes may be attached to aid stability on the ascent. These are not essential to performance but will enhance appearance.

Test for lift-off in your garage, then away to the open spaces. Get a willing helper to support the rocket by its loop on the end of an old fishing rod or garden cane having, of course, found a favourable sheltered spot for your launching pad. Then fuel up and ignite. The calmer the day, the more realistic the ascent. Should the model tilt in flight, add a small amount of weight to the hoop to keep the model vertical. Bulldog clips are ideal for this purpose. Much depends on weight of tissue

(a) Join vertical seam to form cylindrical Rocket body

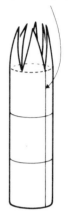

(b) Complete nose cone by seaming the six triangular red panels, adding string loop and tissue disc for suspension at top

Fig 27 Seaming and completion of Rocket body

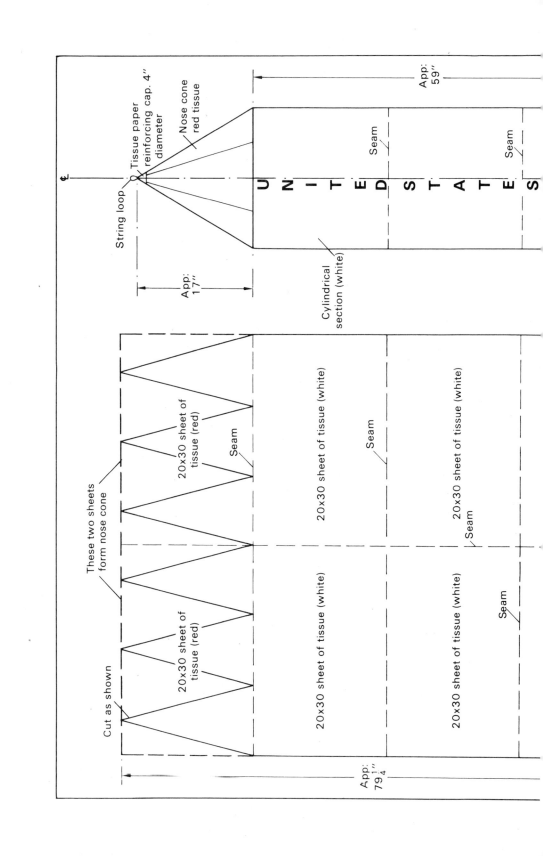

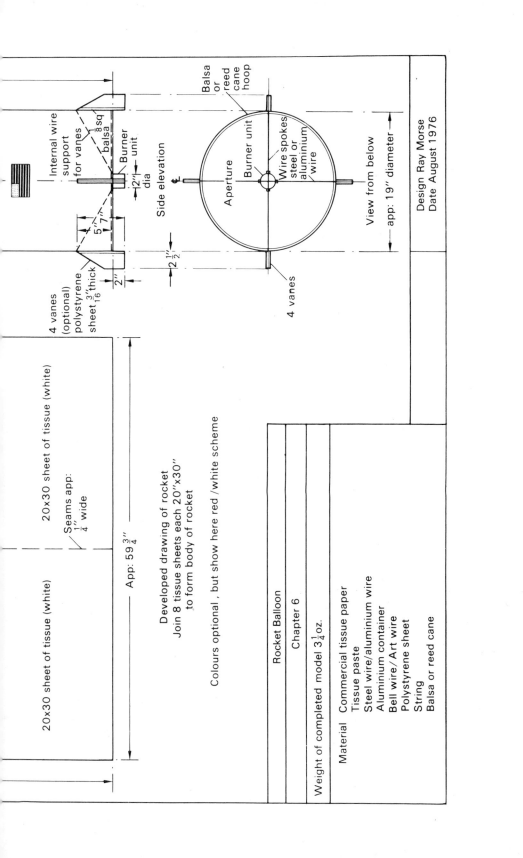

20x30 sheet of tissue (white)

20x30 sheet of tissue (white)

Seams app: $\frac{1}{4}''$ wide

App: 59 $\frac{3}{4}''$

Developed drawing of rocket
Join 8 tissue sheets each 20''x30''
to form body of rocket

Colours optional , but show here red /white scheme

4 vanes
(optional)
polystyrene
sheet $\frac{3}{16}''$ thick

$2''$

$2\frac{1}{2}''$

Internal wire
support
for vanes

$\frac{1}{8}$ sq
balsa

Burner
unit

$2''$
dia

$5'' 7''$

Side elevation

Balsa
or
reed
cane
hoop

Burner unit

Aperture

Wire spokes
steel or
aluminium
wire

View from below

app: 19'' diameter

4 vanes

Rocket Balloon

Chapter 6

Weight of completed model $3\frac{1}{4}$ oz.

Material   Commercial tissue paper
Tissue paste
Steel wire/aluminium wire
Aluminium container
Bell wire/ Art wire
Polystyrene sheet
String
Balsa or reed cane

Design Ray Morse
Date August 1976

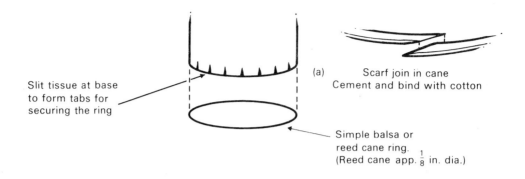

Slit tissue at base
to form tabs for
securing the ring

(a)

Scarf join in cane
Cement and bind with cotton

Simple balsa or
reed cane ring.
(Reed cane app. $\frac{1}{8}$ in. dia.)

Fig 28 (a) A simple ring for fireless rocket

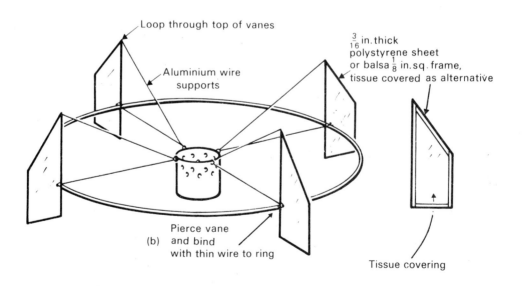

Loop through top of vanes

Aluminium wire
supports

$\frac{3}{16}$ in. thick
polystyrene sheet
or balsa $\frac{1}{8}$ in. sq. frame,
tissue covered as alternative

Tissue covering

(b)

Pierce vane
and bind
with thin wire to ring

Fig 28 (b) Burner unit and vanes added
Burner same pattern as for 1930s model (Fig 15)

and amount of glue you have used. It is surprising the extent to which the performance of a model aeroplane will vary due to the quantity of cement the modeller has used. Thus, quite often, two identical models, built to the same plans, will require different trim to give good flying results. The same applies, too, to the weight of paints or dopes on a model, a point not always realized by a beginner.

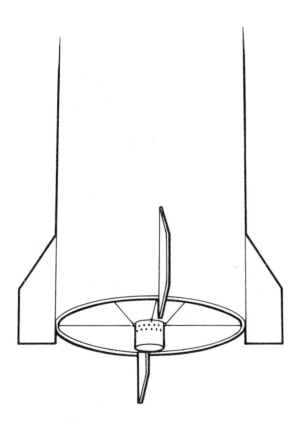

Fig 29 View of underside showing burner unit and vanes

Do please remember dry grass or crops when using methylated spirits. Fire brigades have more than enough to do without additional hazards.

Successful lift-offs and 'soft' landings!
Three, two, one, zero!

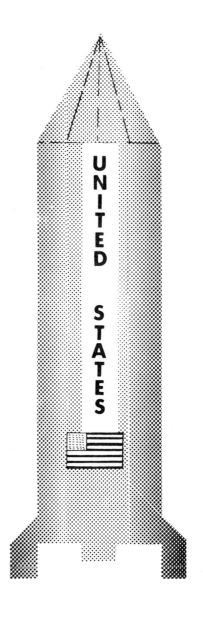

Chapter 7
La Montgolfière

As a fitting tribute to the two famous French brothers, Joseph and Etienne Montgolfier, who actually invented the hot-air balloon (by holding paper bags over a chafing-dish) during the 1780s, I am happy to include a miniature version of this notable machine in this book. I have found that the model behaves just as well as the full-size counterpart of 1783, so why not try to commemorate also, by including this colourful balloon in your aerial fleet?

Basically, construction varies little from my other examples, apart from incorporation of the gallery, used so frequently in those early days instead of the more familiar basket invariably fitted nowadays to hold the crew.

As with most of the previous balloons, start by cutting out a stiff paper template to pattern as shown, then glue sufficient blue tissue sheets together to make the eight gores, or panels, of the canopy. A longitudinal crease both on template and tissues will help when forming pile (template on top). Temporarily pin the lot together then, following the curvature of the template, cut out the pile, separate, and start pasting the panels together, in pairs as shown. Lay two panels flat on bench with $\frac{3}{8}$-in. offset sideways. Run glue brush along edge of top panel, then fold projecting dry edge of lower panel over on to it, forming seam.

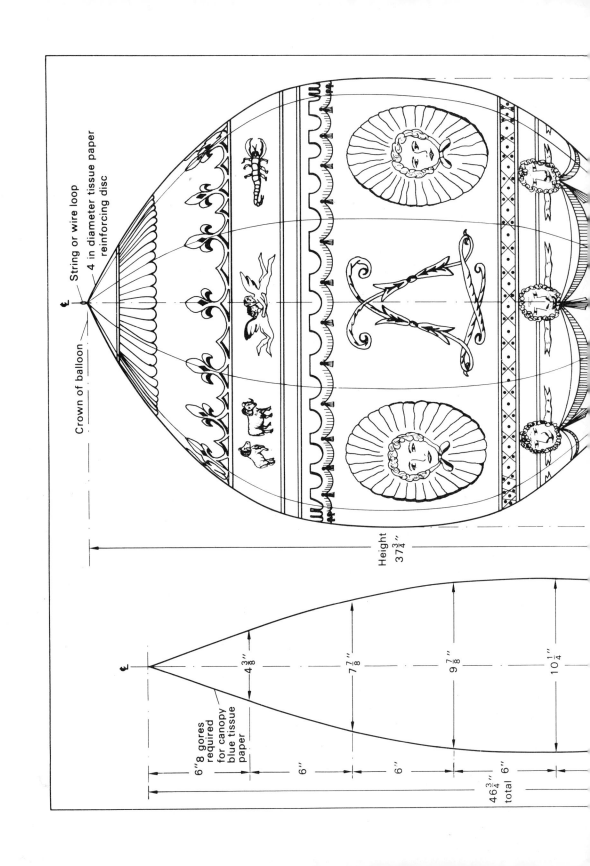

Crown of balloon

String or wire loop

4 in diameter tissue paper reinforcing disc

Height 37¾"

4³⁄₈"

7⁷⁄₈"

9⁷⁄₈"

10¼"

6"8 gores required for canopy blue tissue paper

6"

6"

6"

46³⁄₄" total

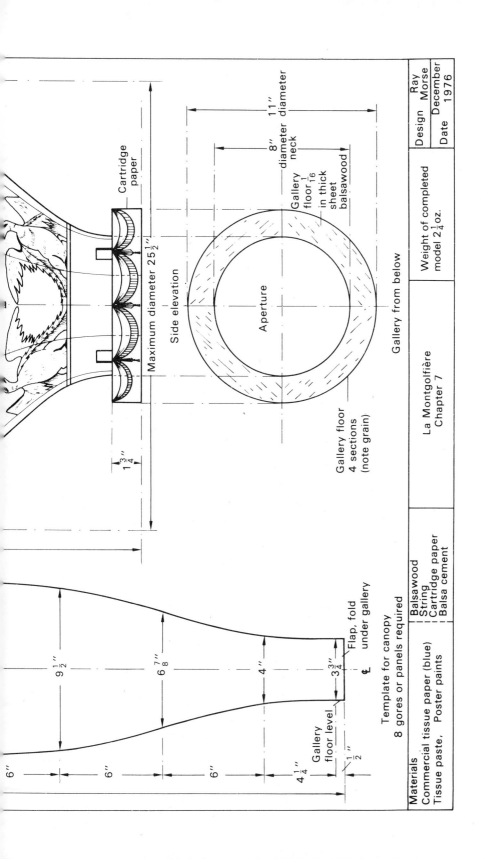

Cartridge paper

Maximum diameter $25\frac{1}{2}''$

Side elevation

$1\frac{3}{4}''$

$8''$ diameter neck

$11''$ diameter

Gallery floor $\frac{1}{16}$ in thick sheet balsawood

Aperture

Gallery floor
4 sections
(note grain)

Gallery from below

Template for canopy
8 gores or panels required

$9\frac{1}{2}''$

$6\frac{7}{8}''$

$4''$

$3\frac{3}{4}''$

Flap, fold under gallery

Gallery
floor level

$4\frac{1}{4}''$

$\frac{1}{2}''$

$6''$

$6''$

$6''$

$6''$

Materials		Balsawood	La Montgolfière	Weight of completed	Design	Ray Morse
Commercial tissue paper (blue)		String	Chapter 7	model $2\frac{1}{4}$ oz.		
Tissue paste. Poster paints		Cartridge paper			Date	December 1976
		Balsa cement				

Repeat by assembling the four pairs then, in turn, form complete canopy by joining these together, eight panels in all. Immediately open to prevent adhesive holding in wrong place, fixing a 4-in. diameter tissue disc to the crown (top) with a string loop in order to suspend balloon during inflation.

At this stage of the work it would be as well to decorate the balloon in the elaborate but gay scheme of King Louis's time, with the suns, signs of the zodiac, eagles and royal ciphers picked out in red and gold on the blue ground; quite a work of art but, nevertheless, provides character of the period. Alternatively, these designs may be cut from thin coloured paper or foil and pasted in position.

Next, tackle the balsa gallery unit – quite a simple structure. Cover this with tissue and attach completed balloon to it as shown.

All is ready for a trial. *La Montgolfière* may be tested in the garage first, or wait for calm weather and find a sheltered corner for your maiden flight outdoors. As usual, get a helper to suspend the deflated model by the crown, held up on the end of a rod by the loop, using a gas picnic stove, as previously mentioned, for inflation purposes. One may even consider a scenic version of this model by building a miniature raised platform from which the actual balloon ascended, as depicted in the early engravings. This platform or staging could house the picnic stove concealed from view, with the model's gallery resting on the top ready for take-off. Miniature card figures in period costume would complete the historic scene. *Vive la France!*

Glossary

AERODYNE   A heavier-than-air craft.

AEROSTAT   A lighter-than-air craft.

APERTURE   The opening or orifice in the underside of a hot-air balloon.

BALLAST   Any substance such as sand or water which can be discharged from a balloon to alter balance.

BALSA   A lightweight timber used much in aircraft work, grown mainly in Equador, South America.

BRACE   A carpenter's handbrace, fitted with chuck, used for drilling, but often adapted for winding rubber motors of model aircraft.

BUOYANCY   The vertical thrust of an aircraft in air, equal to the weight of air displaced.

CANOPY   The envelope of an aerostat in which the gas or hot air is contained.

CEMENT   A type of glue.

CG   Centre of gravity.

₡   Denotes centre-line.

CONCENTRIC	Having a common centre.
CROWN	Top of a balloon. A valve is usually fitted here in a gas balloon.
ENVELOPE	The gas container of a balloon.
EQUILIBRIUM	A state of static balance. When an aerostat is exactly equal to weight of air it displaces.
FRAME (or RING)	Used at neck aperture of a model balloon.
FREE BALLOON	An untethered non-propelled lighter-than-air craft, free to drift with the wind.
FREE FLIGHT	A flying machine free of any form of tether.
GALLERY	The circular type of structure used on early hot-air balloons for accommodating the crew.
GONDOLA	The basket or car of a balloon.
GORE	The panel of a balloon's canopy, a number of which go to form the complete container.
HEAVY	An aerostat in a heavy condition tends to sink.
KITE BALLOON	A captive or tethered balloon shaped to obtain additional lift and stability from the wind, often used for radio aerials and for gathering weather data from higher altitudes. Kite balloons were much used in World War I for observation purposes.
LAP JOIN	An overlap.

LIFT	The upward force acting on an aerostat due to the property of the gas contained therein.
LIGHT	An aerostat in a 'light' condition tends to rise.
LTA	Lighter than air.
SKIRT	A circular belt of fire-resistant fabric fitted to hot-air balloons in the vicinity of the burner on the underside of the canopy.
SWG	Standard Wire Gauge.
TEMPLATE	A template or pattern. Used when a number of parts are required to the same size and shape.
TETHERED FLIGHT	A flight in which the machine is restricted by a line or lines.
TRAIL ROPE	A heavy rope used on balloons to check descent and form a drag whilst landing. Used also for trailing in open country, the rope compensating the rise and fall of the balloon.
VANE	Often used in the control system of rockets.

Index

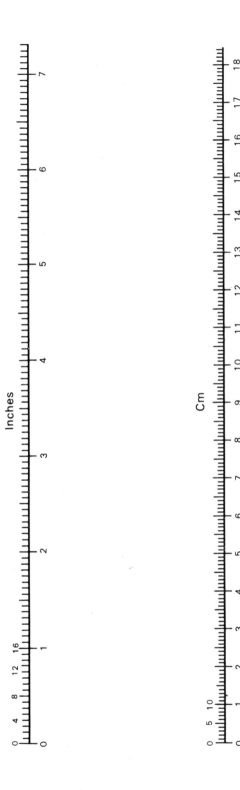

Inches

Cm

62

Legal Standard Wire-Gauge	
Description No.	Equivalent parts of an inch
16	0.064
18	0.048
20	0.036
22	0.028
24	0.022
26	0.018
28	0.014
30	0.013
32	0.010
34	0.009
36	0.007
38	0.006